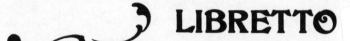

LIBRETTO

The Sorcerer

© 2007 by Faber Music Ltd
First published by International Music Publications Ltd
International Music Publications Ltd is a Faber Music company
3 Queen Square, London WC1N 3AU
Printed in England by Caligraving Ltd
All rights reserved

ISBN10: 0-571-52901-1
EAN13: 978-0-571-52901-8

To buy Faber Music publications or to find out about the full range of titles available,
please contact your local music retailer or Faber Music sales enquiries:

Faber Music Ltd, Burnt Mill, Elizabeth Way, Harlow, CM20 2HX England
Tel: +44(0)1279 82 89 82   Fax: +44(0)1279 82 89 83
sales@fabermusic.com   fabermusic.com

DRAMATIS PERSONAE

SIR MARMADUKE POINTDEXTRE *(an Elderly Baronet)*

ALEXIS *(of the Grenadier Guards—his Son)*

DR. DALY *(Vicar of Ploverleigh)*

NOTARY

JOHN WELLINGTON WELLS *(of J. W. Wells & Co., Family Sorcerers)*

LADY SANGAZURE *(a Lady of Ancient Lineage)*

ALINE *(her Daughter—betrothed to Alexis)*

MRS. PARTLET *(a Pew Opener)*

CONSTANCE *(her Daughter)*

CHORUS OF VILLAGERS

ACT I
Exterior of Sir Marmaduke's Mansion. Mid-day.

(Twelve hours are supposed to elapse between Acts I and II)

ACT II
Exterior of Sir Marmaduke's Mansion. Midnight.

MUSICAL NUMBERS

ACT I

ACT II

THE SORCERER

Act 1

SCENE—*Exterior of Sir Marmaduke's Elizabethan Mansion.*

Music No. 1 CHORUS OF VILLAGERS.

"Ring forth, ye bells"

CHORUS
Ring forth, ye bells,
With clarion sound,
Forget your knells,
For joys abound,
Forget your notes
Of mournful lay,
And from your throats
Pour joy today.

WOMEN	MEN
For young Alexis—	
	Young Alexis Pointdextre,
Is betrothed to Aline,—	
	To Aline Sangazure.
And that pride of his sex is—	
	of his sex is to be next her,
At the feast on the green,—	
	on the green. Oh, be sure!

CHORUS (All)
And that pride of his sex is, of his sex is to be next her,
At the feast on the green, on the green, Oh, be sure!

WOMEN
Ring forth, ye bells,
With clarion sound,

CHORUS (All)
Forget your knells,
For joys abound,
For joys abound,
Forget your knells,
For joys abound.
Ring forth, ye bells,
With clarion sound,
And from your throats
Pour joy today.
Ring forth, ye bells,
With clarion sound,
Forget your knells,
For joys abound.
Ring forth, ye bells,
With clarion sound,
Forget your knells,
For joys abound.

Ring forth, ye bells,
With clarion sound,
Forget your knells,
For joys abound.
Ring, ye bells,
Ring, ye bells,
Ring, ye bells,
With clarion sound,
For joys abound.

(**Exeunt men**)
(**Enter MRS. PARTLET with CONSTANCE, her daughter**)

Music No. 2 RECIT. (Mrs. Partlet and Constance)

"Constance, my daughter, why this strange depression?"

MRS. P.   Constance, my daughter, why this strange depression?
The village rings with seasonable joy,
Because the young and amiable Alexis,
Heir to the great Sir Marmaduke Pointdextre,
Is plighted to Aline, the only daughter
Of Annabella, Lady Sangazure
You, you alone are sad and out of spirits;
What is the reason? Speak, my daughter, speak!

CON.   Oh, mother, do not ask! If my complexion
From red to white should change in quick succession—
And then from white to red, oh, take no notice!
If my poor limbs should tremble with emotion,
Pay no attention, mother—it is nothing!
If long and deep-drawn sighs I chance to utter,
Oh, heed them not, their cause must ne'er be known!

MRS. PARTLET motions to CHORUS to leave her with CONSTANCE.
(**Exeunt girls**)

Music No. 2a ARIA (Constance)

"When he is here"

CON.   When he is here,
I sigh with pleasure,
When he is gone,
I sigh with grief.
My hopeless fear
No soul can measure,
His love alone
Can give my aching heart relief,
Can give my aching heart relief!
When he is cold,
I weep for sorrow,
When he is kind,

CON. (**Contd**)	I weep for joy. My grief untold Knows no tomorrow My grief untold Knows no tomorrow— My woe can find No hope, no solace, no alloy! No hope, no hope, no solace, no alloy! When I rejoice, He shows no pleasure, When I am sad, It grieves him not. His solemn voice Has tones I treasure— My heart they glad, They solace my unhappy lot! They solace my unhappy lot! When I despond, My woe they chasten, When I take heart, My hope they cheer: With folly fond To him I hasten— With folly fond To him I hasten— From him apart, My life is very sad and drear! My life, my life is very sad and drear!
MRS. P.	Come, tell me all about it! Do not fear— I, too, have loved; but that was long ago! Who is the object of your young affections?
CON.	Hush, mother! He is here! (*Looking off*)
MRS. P.	(*Amazed*). Our reverend vicar!
CON.	Oh pity me, my heart is almost broken!
MRS. P.	My child, be comforted. To such an union I shall not offer any opposition. Take him—he's yours! May you and he be happy!
CON.	But, mother dear, he is not yours to give!
MRS. P.	That's true, indeed!
CON.	He might object!
MRS. P.	He might. But come—take heart—I'll probe him on the subject. Be comforted—leave this affair to me. (*They withdraw*)

(Enter DR. DALY. He is pensive and does not see them)

3

Music No. 3 RECIT. (Rev. Dr. Daly)

"The air is charged with amatory numbers"

DR. D.   The air is charged with amatory numbers—
Soft madrigals, and dreamy lovers' lays.
Peace, peace, old heart! Why waken from its slumbers
The aching mem'ry of the old, old days?

Music No. 3a BALLAD (Dr. Daly)

"Time was, when Love and I were well acquainted"

DR. D.   Time was, when Love and I were well acquainted.
Time was, when we walk'd ever hand in hand.
A saintly youth, with worldly thought untainted—
None better-lov'd than I in all the land!
Time was, when maidens of the noblest station,
Forsaking even military men,
Would gaze upon me, rapt in adoration—
Ah me, ah me, I was a fair young curate then!
Had I a head-ache? sigh'd the maids assembled:
Had I a cold? well'd forth the silent tear:
Did I look pale? then half a parish trembled:
And when I cough'd all thought the end was near!
I had no care—no jealous doubts hung o'er me,
For I was lov'd beyond all other men.
Fled gilded dukes and belted earls before me,
Ah me, ah me, I was a pale young curate then!
A pale young curate, a pale young curate,
Ah me, I was a pale young curate then!

**(At the conclusion of the ballad,
MRS. PARTLET comes forward with CONSTANCE)**

MRS. P.   Good day, reverend sir.

DR. D.   Ah, good Mrs. Partlet, I am glad to see you. And your little daughter, Constance! Why, she is quite a little woman, I declare!

CON.   *(aside)*. Oh, mother, I cannot speak to him!

MRS. P.   Yes, reverend sir, she is nearly eighteen, and as good a girl as ever stepped. *(Aside to* Dr. D.) Ah, sir, I'm afraid I shall soon lose her!

DR. D.   *(aside to* Mrs. P.). Dear me, you pain me very much. Is she delicate?

MRS. P.   Oh no, sir—I don't mean that—but young girls look to get married.

DR. D.   Oh, I take you. To be sure. But there's plenty of time for that. Four or five years hence, Mrs. Partlet, four or five years hence. But when the time *does* come, I shall have much pleasure in marrying her myself—

CON.   *(aside)*. Oh, mother!

DR. D.	To some strapping young fellow in her own rank of life.
CON.	*(in tears)*. He does *not* love me!
MRS. P.	I have often wondered, reverend sir (if you'll excuse the liberty), that *you* have never married.
DR. D.	*(aside)*. Be still my fluttering heart!
MRS. P.	A clergyman's wife does so much good in a village. Besides that, you are not as young as you were, and before very long you will want somebody to nurse you, and look after your little comforts.
DR. D.	Mrs. Partlet, there is much truth in what you say. I am indeed getting on in years, and a help-mate would cheer my declining days. Time was when it might have been; but I have left it too long—I am an old fogy now, am I not, my dear? *(to Constance)*—a very old fogy, indeed. Ha! ha! No, Mrs. Partlet, my mind is quite made up. I shall live and die a solitary old bachelor.
CON.	Oh, mother, mother! *(Sobs on* Mrs. Partlet's *bosom)*.
MRS P.	Come, come, dear one, don't fret. At a more fitting time we will try again—we will try again.

(Exeunt MRS. PARTLET and CONSTANCE)

DR. D.	*(looking after them)*. Poor little girl! I'm afraid she has something on her mind. She is rather comely. Time was when this old heart would have throbbed in double-time at the sight of such a fairy form! But tush! I am puling! Here comes the young Alexis with his proud and happy father. Let me dry this tell-tale tear!

Enter SIR MARMADUKE and ALEXIS

Music No. 4 RECIT. and MINUET (Sir Marmaduke, Dr. Daly, and Alexis)

"Sir Marmaduke, my dear young friend, Alexis"

RECITATIVE

DR. D.	Sir Marmaduke—my dear young friend, Alexis— On this most happy—most auspicious plighting— Permit me, as a true friend, to tender My best, my very best congratulations!
SIR M.	Sir, you are most obleeging!
ALEXIS	Dr. Daly, My dear old tutor, and my valued pastor, I thank you from the bottom of my heart!

(Spoken through music)

DR. D.	May fortune bless you! may the middle distance Of your young life be pleasant as the foreground— The joyous foreground! and, when you have reached it, May that which now is the far-off horizon (But which will then become the middle distance), In fruitful promise be exceeded only By that which will have opened, in the meantime, Into a new and glorious horizon!
SIR M.	Dear Sir, that is an excellent example Of an old school of stately compliment To which I have, through life, been much addicted. Will you obleege me with a copy of it, In clerkly manuscript, that I myself May use it on appropriate occasions?
DR. D.	Sir, you shall have a fairly-written copy Ere Sol has sunk into his western slumbers!

(Exit DR. DALY)

SIR M.	*(to Alexis, who is in a reverie)*. Come, come, my son—your *fiancée* will be here in five minutes. Rouse yourself to receive her.
ALEXIS	Oh rapture!
SIR M.	Yes, you are a fortunate young fellow, and I will not disguise from you that this union with the House of Sangazure realizes my fondest wishes. Aline is rich, and she comes of a sufficiently old family, for she is the seven thousand and thirty-seventh in direct descent from Helen of Troy. True, there was a blot on the escutcheon of that lady—that affair with Paris—but where is the family, other than my own, in which there is no flaw? You are a lucky fellow, sir—a very lucky fellow!
ALEXIS	Father, I am welling over with limpid joy! No sicklying taint of sorrow overlies the lucid lake of liquid love, upon which, hand-in-hand, Aline and I are to float into eternity!
SIR M.	Alexis, I desire that of your love for this young lady you do not speak so openly. You are always singing ballads in praise of her beauty, and you expect the very menials who wait behind your chair to chorus your ecstasies. It is not delicate.
ALEXIS	Father, a man who loves as I love—
SIR M.	Pooh pooh, sir! thirty years so ago I madly loved your future mother-in-law, the Lady Sangazure, and I have reason to believe that she returned my love. But were we guilty of the indelicacy of publicly rushing into each other's arms, exclaiming— "Oh my adored one!" "Beloved boy!" "Ecstatic rapture!" "Unmingled joy!" which seems to be the modern fashion of love-making? No! it was "Madam, I trust you are in the enjoyment of good health"—"Sir, you are vastly polite, I protest I am mighty well"—and so forth. Much more delicate—much more respectful. But see—Aline approaches—let us retire, that she may compose herself for the interesting ceremony in which she is to play so important a part.

6

Exeunt SIR MARMADUKE and ALEXIS.
Enter ALINE, on terrace, preceded by chorus of girls.

Music No. 5 CHORUS OF GIRLS

"With heart and with voice"

CHORUS   With heart and with voice
Let us welcome this mating
To the youth of her choice:
With a heart palpitating,
Comes the lovely Aline!
Comes the lovely Aline!
May their love never cloy!
May their bliss be unbounded!
With a halo of joy
May their lives be surrounded!
Heaven bless our Aline!
Heaven bless our Aline!
May their love never cloy!
May their bliss be unbounded!
With a halo of joy
May their lives be surrounded!
Heaven bless Aline!
May their love never cloy!
May their bliss be unbounded!
Heaven bless our Aline! . . . . . bless our Aline!
Heaven bless our Aline!
Heaven bless our Aline! bless our Aline!

Music No. 6 RECIT. (Aline)

"My kindly friends"

ALINE   My kindly friends, I thank you for this greeting,
And as you wish me ev'ry earthly joy,
I trust your wishes may have quick fulfilment!

Music No. 6a ARIA (Aline)

"Happy young heart"

ALINE   Oh, happy young heart!
Comes thy young lord a-wooing
With joy in his eyes,
And pride in his breast—
Make much of thy prize,
For he is the best
That ever came a-suing,
That ever came a-suing.
Yet, yet we must part, Young heart!
Yet we must part,
Yet, yet we must part, Young heart!

7

Yet we must part!
Oh, merry young heart,
Bright are the days of wooing!
But happier far
The day untried—
No sorrow can mar,
When Love has tied
The knot there's no un-doing,
There's no un-doing.
Then, never to part, Young heart!
never to part, never to part,
Then, never to part, Young heart!
never to part, never to part, never to part,
never, never, never to part!
never to part, Young heart! to part!

(**Enter LADY SANGAZURE**)

Music No. 7 RECIT. (Lady Sangazure)

"My child, I join in these congratulations"

LADY S.   My child, I join in these congratulations:
Heed not the tear that dims this aged eye!
Old mem'ries crowd around me: Tho' I sorrow,
'Tis for myself, Aline and not for thee!

(**Enter ALEXIS, preceded by Chorus of Men**)

Music No. 8 CHORUS OF MEN

"With heart and with voice"

CHORUS   With heart and with voice
Let us welcome this mating:
To the maid of his choice,
With a heart palpitating.
Comes Alexis the brave!
With heart and with voice
Let us welcome this mating
To the maid of his choice:
To the maid of his choice
Comes the brave Alexis,
The brave Alexis,
Alexis the brave.

**SIR MARMADUKE enters. LADY SANGAZURE and he exhibit signs of
strong emotion at the sight of each other which they endeavour to
repress. ALEXIS and ALINE rush into each other's arms.**

RECITATIVE

ALEXIS   Oh, my adored one!

8

ALINE	Beloved boy!
ALEXIS	Ecstatic rapture!
ALINE	Unmingled joy! *(They retire up)*

Music No. 9 DUET (Lady Sangazure and Sir Marmaduke)

"Welcome, joy!"

SIR M.	*(with stately courtesy)*
	Welcome joy, adieu to sadness!
	As Aurora gilds the day,
	So those eyes, twin orbs of gladness,
	Chase the clouds of care away.
	Irresistible incentive
	Bids me humbly kiss your hand;
	I'm your servant most attentive—
	Most attentive to command!
	(aside with frantic vehemence)
	Wild with adoration!
	Mad with fascination!
	To indulge my lamentation
	No occasion do I miss!
	Goaded to distraction
	By maddening inaction,
	I find some satisfaction
	In apostrophe like this:
	"Sangazure immortal,
	"Sangazure divine,
	"Welcome to my portal
	"Angel, oh be mine!"
	Immortal, divine!
	Angel, oh be mine!"
	(Aloud, with much ceremony)
	Irresistible incentive
	Bids me humbly kiss your hand;
	I'm your servant most attentive—
	Most attentive to command!
LADY S.	Sir, I thank you most politely
	For your graceful courtesee;
	Compliment more truly knightly
	Never yet was paid to me!
	Chivalry is an ingredient
	Sadly lacking in our land—
	Sir, I am your most obedient,
	Most obedient to command!
	(Aside, with great vehemence)
	Wild with adoration!
	Mad with fascination!

To indulge my lamentation
No occasion do I miss!
Goaded to distraction
By maddening inaction,
I find some satisfaction
In apostrophe like this:
"Marmaduke immortal,
"Marmaduke divine,
"Take me to thy portal,
"Loved one, oh be mine!"
Immortal, divine!
Loved one, oh be mine!

LADY S. (*Aloud, with much ceremony*)   **SIR M.** (*aside*)

LADY S.	SIR M.
Chi-	
val-	
ry	Wild with ado-
is	ration!
an	Mad with fasci-
in-	nation! To in-
gre-	dulge my lamen-
dient	tation No oc-
Sadly	casion do I
lack-	miss!
ing	Wild with ado-
in	ration! To in-
our	dulge my lamen-
land.	tation No oc-
	casion do I miss!
	(*Aloud*)
(*Aside*)	I'm
Wild with ado-	your
ration!	ser-
Mad with fasci-	vant
nation! To in-	most
dulge my lamen-	at-
tation No oc-	ten-
casion do I	tive,
miss!	Most atten---
To in-	--------
dulge my lamen-	tive
tation, No occasion	to
do I	com-
miss!	mand!

BOTH   (*aside*) Wild with adoration,
Yes, and mad with fascination!
To indulge my lamentation
No occasion do I miss!
(*aloud*) Your most obedient!
Your most obedient to command.

(During this the NOTARY has entered, with marriage contract)

Music No. 10 ENSEMBLE (Aline, Alexis, Lawyer, and Chorus)

"All is prepared"

LAWYER   All is prepar'd for sealing and for signing,
          The contract has been drafted as agreed.

CHORUS   All is prepar'd for sealing and for signing,
          The contract has been drafted as agreed!

LAWYER   Approach the table, Oh ye lovers pining!
          With hand and seal now execute the deed!

CHORUS   Approach the table, Oh ye lovers pining,
          With hand and seal come execute the deed.

**(ALEXIS and ALINE advance and sign,
ALEXIS supported by SIR MARMADUKE, ALINE by her Mother)**

ALEXIS   I deliver it, I deliver it,
          As my act and deed.

ALINE   I deliver it, I deliver it,
          As my act and deed.

CHORUS   See, they sign without a quiver!
          It then to seal proceed!
          They deliver it, They deliver it,
          As their act and deed!

ALL   I / They   deliver it,   I / They   deliver it,

     As my / their   act and deed.

CHORUS

WOMEN	MEN
	With heart and with voice Let
With heart and with voice	us welcome this mating;
Let us welcome this	Leave them here to re-
mating;	joice,
Leave them here to re-	With true love palpi-
joice,	tating,
With	
true love	A---
pal-	lex-
pi-	is the
tating,	brave!
	With heart
Leave them	
here	and with voice
to re-	

CHORUS	WOMEN (Contd)	MEN
	joice,	Let us wel-
	With true love	come
		this ma-
	palpi-	-----
	ta-	
	ting;	ting!
	Heaven	Leave them
	bless our A-	here to re-
	line!	joice, Leave them
	The lovely Aline!	here to rejoice,
	Alexis the brave	Alexis the brave!
	And the lovely Aline!	Alexis the brave
		And the lovely Aline!

(Exeunt all but ALEXIS and ALINE)

ALEXIS   At last we are alone! My darling, you are now irrevocably betrothed to me. Are you not very, very happy?

ALINE   Oh, Alexis, can you doubt it? Do I not love you beyond all on earth, and am I not beloved in return? Is not true love, faithfully given and faithfully returned, the source of every earthly joy?

ALEXIS   Of that there can be no doubt. Oh, that the world could be persuaded of the truth of that maxim! Oh, that the world would break down the artificial barriers of rank, wealth, education, age, beauty, habits, taste, and temper, and recognise the glorious principle, that in marriage alone is to be found the panacea for every ill.

ALINE   Continue to preach that sweet doctrine, and you will suceed, oh evangel of true happiness!

ALEXIS   I hope so, but as yet the cause progresses but slowly. Still I have made some converts to the principle, that men and women should be coupled in matrimony without distinction of rank. I have lectured on the subject at Mechanics' Institutes, and the mechanics were unanimous in favour of my views. I have preached in workhouses, beershops, and Lunatic Asylums, and I have been received with enthusiasm. I have addressed navvies on the advantages that would accrue to them if they married wealthy ladies of rank, and not a navvy dissented!

ALINE   Noble fellows! And yet there are those who hold that the uneducated classes are not open to argument! And what do the countesses say?

ALEXIS   Why, at present, it can't be denied, the aristocracy hold aloof.

ALINE   Ah, the working man is the true Intelligence after all!

ALEXIS   He is a noble creature when he is quite sober. Yes, Aline, true happiness comes of true love, and true love should be independent of external influences. It should live upon itself and by itself—in itself love should live for love alone!

12

Music No. 11 BALLAD (Alexis)

"For Love alone"

ALEXIS
Love feeds on many kinds of food, I know;
Some love for rank, and some for duty;
Some give their hearts away for empty show,
And others love for youth and beauty.
To love for money all the world is prone;
Some love themselves, and live all lonely:
Give me the love that loves for love alone—
I love that love, I love it only!
I love that love, I love it only!
Give me the love that loves for love alone—
I love that love, I love it only!
What man for any other joy can thirst,
Whose loving wife adores him duly?
Want, misery, and care may work their worst,
If loving woman loves you truly.
A lover's thoughts are ever with his own—
None truly lov'd is ever lonely:
Give me the love that loves for love alone—
I love that love, I love it only!
I love that love, I love it only!
Give me the love that loves for love alone—
I love that love, I love it only!

ALINE
Oh, Alexis, those are noble principles!

ALEXIS
Yes, Aline, and I am going to take a desperate step in support of them. Have you ever heard of the firm of J. W. Wells & Co., the old established Family Sorcerers in St. Mary Axe?

ALINE
I have seen their advertisement.

ALEXIS
They have invented a philtre, which, if report may be believed, is simply infallible. I intend to distribute it through the village, and within half an hour of my doing so there will not be an adult in the place who will not have learnt the secret of pure and lasting happiness. What do you say to that?

ALINE
Well, dear, of course a filter is a very useful thing in a house; but still I don't quite see that it is the sort of thing that places its possessor on the very pinnacle of earthly joy.

ALEXIS
Aline, you misunderstand me. I didn't say a filter—I said a philtre.

ALINE
(alarmed). You don't mean a love-potion?

ALEXIS
On the contrary—I *do* mean a love-potion.

ALINE
Oh Alexis! I don't think it would be right. I don't indeed. And then—a real magician! Oh, it would be downright wicked.

13

ALEXIS	Aline, is it, or is it not, a laudable object to steep the whole village up to its lips in love, and to couple them in matrimony without distinction of age, rank, or fortune?
ALINE	Unquestionably, but—
ALEXIS	Then, unpleasant as it must be to have recourse to supernatural aid, I must nevertheless pocket my aversion, in deference to the great and good end I have in view. *(Calling)* Hercules.

Enter a Page from tent.

PAGE	Yes, sir.
ALEXIS	Is Mr. Wells there?
PAGE	He's in the tent, sir—refreshing.
ALEXIS	Ask him to be so good as to step this way.
PAGE	Yes, sir. *(Exit Page)*.
ALINE	Oh, but Alexis! A real Sorcerer! Oh. I shall be frightened to death!
ALEXIS	I trust my Aline will not yield to fear while the strong right arm of her Alexis is here to protect her.
ALINE	It's nonsense, dear, to talk of your protecting me with your strong right arm, in face of the fact that this Family Sorcerer could change me into a guinea-pig before you could turn round.
ALEXIS	He *could* change you into a guinea-pig, no doubt, but it is most unlikely that he would take such a liberty. It's a most respectable firm, and I am sure he would never be guilty of so untradesmanlike an act.

Enter MR WELLS from tent.

MR. W.	Good day, sir. (ALINE *much terrified*).
ALEXIS	Good day—I believe you are a Sorcerer.
MR. W.	Yes, sir, we practise Necromancy in all its branches. We've a choice assortment of wishing-caps, divining-rods, amulets, charms, and counter-charms. We can cast you a nativity at a low figure, and we have a horoscope at three-and-six that we can guarantee. Our Abudah chests, each containing a patent Hag who comes out and prophesies disasters, with spring complete, are strongly recommended. Our Aladdin lamps are very chaste, and our Prophetic Tablets, foretelling everything—from a change of Ministry down to a rise in Unified—are much enquired for. Our penny Curse—one of the cheapest things in the trade—is considered infallible. We have some very superior Blessings, too, but they're very little asked for. We've only sold one since Christmas—to a gentleman who bought it to send to his mother-in-law—but it turned out that he was afflicted in the head, and it's been returned on our hands. But our sale of penny Curses, especially on Saturday nights, is tremendous. We can't turn 'em out fast enough.

Music No. 12 SONG (Mr. Wells)

"My name is John Wellington Wells"

MR. WELLS   My name is John Wellington Wells,
I'm a dealer in magic and spells,
In blessings and curses,
And ever-fill'd purses,
In prophecies, witches, and knells.
If you want a proud foe to "make tracks"—
If you'd melt a rich uncle in wax—
You've but to look in
On the resident Djinn,
Number seventy, Simmery Axe!
We've a first-class assortment of magic;
And for raising a posthumous shade
With effects that are comic or tragic,
There's no cheaper house in the trade.
Love-philtre—we've quantities of it;
And for knowledge if any one burns,
We're keeping a very small prophet, a prophet
Who brings us unbounded returns:
For he can prophesy
With a wink *of* his eye,
Peep with security
Into futurity,
Sum up your history,
Clear up a mystery,
Humour proclivity
For a nativity—for a nativity;
He has answers oracular.
Bogies spectacular,
Tetrapods tragical,
Mirrors so magical,
Facts astronomical,
Solemn or comical,
And, if you want it, he
Makes a reduction on taking a quantity!
Oh!
If anyone anything lacks,
He'll find it all ready in stacks.
If he'll only look in
On the resident Djinn,
Number seventy, Simmery Axe!
He can raise you hosts
Of ghosts,
And that, without reflectors;
And creepy things
With wings,
And gaunt and grisly spectres
He can fill you crowds
Of shrouds,
And horrify you vastly;

15

MR. WELLS	He can rack your brains
(Contd)	With chains,
	And gibberings grim and ghastly!
	Then, if you plan it, he
	Changes organity,
	With an urbanity,
	Full of Satanity,
	Vexes humanity
	With an inanity
	Fatal to vanity—
	Driving your foes to the verge of insanity!
	Barring tautology,
	In demonology,
	'Lectro biology,
	Mystic nosology,
	Spirit philology,
	High-class astrology,
	Such is his knowledge, he
	Isn't the man to require an apology!
	Oh!
	My name is John Wellington Wells,
	I'm a dealer in magic and spells,
	In blessings and curses,
	And ever-fill'd purses—
	In prophecies, witches, and knells.
	And if anyone anything lacks,
	He'll find it all ready in stacks,
	If he'll only look in
	On the resident Djinn,
	Number seventy, Simmery Axe!

ALEXIS I have sent for you to consult you on a very important matter. I believe you advertise a Patent Oxy-Hydrogen Love-at-first-sight Philtre?

MR. WELLS Sir, it is our leading article. *(Producing a phial)*.

ALEXIS Now I want to know if you can confidently guarantee it as possessing all the qualities you claim for it in your advertisement?

MR. WELLS Sir, we are not in the habit of puffing our goods. Ours is an old-established house with a large family connection, and every assurance held out in the advertisement is fully realised. *(Hurt)*.

ALINE *(aside)*. Oh, Alexis, don't offend him. He'll change us into something dreadful— I know he will!

ALEXIS I am anxious from purely philanthropical motives to distribute this philtre, secretly, among inhabitants of this village. I shall, of course, require a quantity. How do you sell it?

MR. WELLS In buying a quantity, sir, we should strongly advise your taking it in the wood, and drawing it off as you happen to want it. We have it in four-and-a-half and nine gallon caks—also in pipes and hogsheads for laying down, and we deduct 10 per cent. for prompt cash.

ALEXIS	I should mention that I am a Member of the Army and Navy Stores.

MR. WELLS	In that case we deduct 25 per cent.

ALEXIS	Aline, the villagers will assemble to carouse in a few minutes. Go and fetch the tea-pot.

ALINE	But, Alexis—

ALEXIS	My dear, you must obey me, if you please. Go and fetch the tea-pot.

ALINE	*(Going)*. I'm sure Dr. Daly would disapprove of it!

(Exit ALINE)

ALEXIS	And how soon does it take effect?

MR. WELLS	In twelve hours. Whoever drinks of it loses consciousness for a period, and on waking falls in love, as a matter of course, with the first lady he meets who has also tasted it, and his affection is at once returned. One trial will prove the fact.

(Enter ALINE with large tea-pot)

ALEXIS	Good: then, Mr. Wells, I shall feel obliged if you will at once pour as much philtre into this tea-pot as will suffice to affect the whole village.

ALINE	But bless me, Alexis, many of the villagers are married people!

MR. WELLS	Madam, this philtre is compounded on the strictest principles. On married people it has no effect whatever. But are you quite sure that you have nerve enough to carry you through the fearful ordeal?

ALEXIS	In the good cause I fear nothing.

MR. WELLS	Very good, then, we will proceed at once to the Incantation.

(The stage grows dark)

Music No. 13 INCANTATION (Aline, Alexis, Mr. Wells, and Chorus)

"Sprites of earth and air"

INCANTATION

MR. WELLS	Sprites of earth and air—
	Fiends of flame and fire—
	Demon souls,
	Come here in shoals,
	This dreadful deed inspire!
	Appear, appear, appear

MALE VOICES	Good master, we are here!

MR. WELLS Noisome hags of night—
Imps of deadly shade—
Pallid ghosts,
Arise in hosts,
And lend me all your aid.
Appear, appear, appear!

FEMALE VOICES Good master, we are here!

ALEXIS *(aside).* Hark! hark! they assemble,
These fiends of the night!

ALINE *(aside).* Oh Alexis, I tremble,
Seek safety in flight!

ARIA—ALINE

Let us fly to a far-off land,
Where peace and plenty dwell—
Where the sigh of the silver strand
Is echoed in ev'ry shell.
To the joys that land will give,
On the wings of Love we'll fly;
In innocence there to live—
In innocence there to die!
In innocence there to live,
There to die, to live and die.

ALINE, ALEXIS, MR. WELLS

Too late! too late!

It may not be!

That happy fate
is not for thee!

CHORUS

Too late! too late!

That may not be!

That happy fate is not for thee, ----
----
is not for thee!

MR. WELLS Now shrivelled hags, with poison bags,
Discharge your loathsome loads!
Spit flame and fire, unholy choir!
Belch forth your venom, toads!
Ye demons fell, with yelp and yell,
Shed curses far a-field—
Ye fiends of night, your filthy blight
In noisome plenty yield!

MR. WELLS *(pouring vial into tea-pot—flash).*
Number One!

CHORUS It is done!

MR. WELLS *(same business).* Number Two! *(flash).*

CHORUS   One too few!

MR. WELLS *(same business).* Number Three! *(flash).*

CHORUS   Set us free!
Set us free—our work is done.
Ha! ha! ha!
Ha! ha! ha! ha! ha! ha! ha! ha!

ALINE	ALEXIS	MR. WELLS	CHORUS
Let us fly to a	Let us fly to a		
far off land,	far off land,		
Where peace	Where peace		
and	and		Set us
plen-	plen-		free!
ty	ty		Set us
dwell,	dwell,		free!
		Too late!	
Where the	Where the	too	
sigh of the silver	sigh of the silver	late!	
strand Is e-	strand Is e-		
choed in ev'-	choed in ev'-		Set us free!
ry	ry		set us
shell.	shell.		free!
		Too late!	ha! ha!
Let			ha!
us		too	
fly!		late!	Ha!
	Let us	too	
	fly!	late!	
let us		too	ha!
fly!		late!	ha!
	let us	It	
	fly!	may	
let us		not	ha!
fly!		be!	ha!
	let us	That	
	fly!	hap-	
let us		py	ha!
fly!		fate	ha!
let us	let us	is	ha!
fly!	fly!	not	ha!
let us	let us	for	ha!
fly!	fly!	thee!	ha!

(Stage grows light. MR. WELLS beckons villagers. Enter villagers and all the dramatis personae, dancing joyously. MRS. PARTLET and MR. WELLS then distribute tea-cups.)

Music No. 14 FINALE

"Now to the Banquet we press"

CHORUS   Now to the banquet we press,
Now for the eggs and the ham!
Now for the mustard and cress,
Now for the strawberry jam!
Now for the tea of our host!
Now for the rollicking bun,
Now for the muffin and toast,
And now for the gay Sally Lunn!
Now for the muffin and toast,
And now for the gay Sally Lunn!
The eggs and the ham
And the strawberry jam,
The rollicking bun
And the gay Sally Lunn!

SOPRANOS	ALTOS, TENORS, BASSES
The	The
eggs------	eggs and the ham
----------	And the strawberry jam,
and	
the	The
ham, -------	rollicking bun
	And the gay Sally Lunn!

CHORUS·   The eggs and the ham
And the strawberry jam,
And the rollicking bun!
The rollicking bun
And the gay Sally Lunn
And the strawberry jam,

WOMEN   jam,

MEN   bun,

WOMEN   jam,

MEN   bun,

CHORUS   Oh! the strawberry, strawberry jam,

WOMEN   bun,

MEN   jam

WOMEN   bun,

MEN   jam,

CHORUS   Oh! the rollicking, rollicking bun!

RECIT.—SIR MARMADUKE

Be happy all—the feast is spread before ye,
Fear nothing, but enjoy yourselves, I pray!
Eat, aye, and drink—be merry, I implore ye,
For once let thoughtless Folly rule the day.

TEA-CUP BRINDISI, 1st Verse

Eat, drink, and be gay,
Banish all worry and sorrow,
Laugh gaily to-day,
Weep, (if you're sorry) to-morrow!
Come, pass the cup round—
I will go bail for the liquor;
It's strong, I'll be bound,
For it was brew'd by the vicar!
It's strong, I'll be bound,
For it was brew'd by the vicar!

ALL

None so knowing as he
At brewing a jorum of tea,
Ha! ha! ha! ha!
A pretty stiff jorum of tea.

TRIO—MR. WELLS, ALINE, and ALEXIS (aside)

See! see - they drink,
All thought unheeding,
The tea-cups clink,
They are exceeding!
Their hearts will melt
In half an hour—
Then will be felt
The potion's pow'r!
Then will be felt
The potion's pow'r!
The potion's pow'r!

(During this verse CONSTANCE has brought a small tea-pot, kettle, caddy, and cosy to DR. DALY. He makes tea scientifically)

BRINDISI, 2nd Verse—DR. DALY (with the tea-pot)

Pain, trouble and care,
Misery, heart-ache and worry,
Quick, out of your lair!
Get you all gone in a hurry!
Toil, sorrow and plot,
Fly away quicker and quicker—
Three spoons to the pot—
That is the brew of your vicar!
Three spoons to the pot,
That is the brew of your vicar!

21

ALL	None so cunning as he At brewing a jorum of tea, Ha! ha! ha! ha! A pretty stiff jorum of tea!

ENSEMBLE—ALEXIS and ALINE (aside)

BOTH	Oh love, true love! Unworldly, abiding! Source of all pleasure, true fountain of joy, Oh love, true love, divinely confiding, Exquisite treasure that knows no alloy!
ALEXIS	Oh love, true love, rich harvest of gladness, Peace-bearing tillage, great garner of bliss, Oh love,
ALINE	Oh love,
BOTH	Oh love, Oh love, true love, look down on our sadness, Dwell in this village,

ALINE	**ALEXIS**
Oh dwell in this village, oh hear, ------	Dwell in this village,
---------------	oh hear us,
oh hear ------- us,	Oh hear us in this
	Oh
Hear----- us, oh love, in this!	hear us, oh hear us, oh hear-- us, love, in this!

BOTH	Oh love, true love, oh hear us in this!

It becomes evident by the strange conduct of the characters that the charm is working. All rub their eyes, and stagger about the stage as if under the influence of a narcotic)

DR. D., SIR M., NOTARY, TENORS & BASSES

Oh marvellous illusion!
Oh terrible surprise!
What is this strange confusion
That veils my aching eyes?

ALINE, ALEXIS, MR. WELLS

A marvellous illusion,
A terrible surprise
Excites a strange confusion
Within their aching eyes-

ALL (aside) They/I must regain their/my senses,
Restoring reason's law,
Or fearful inferences
The company will draw!
Or fearful inferences
The company will draw!

ALINE & CON.

Oh
marvel-
lous il-
usion!
Oh
terri-
ble sur-
prise! Oh
mar--
vel-
lous ----

--Oh
mar-vel-
lous illusion!

Oh
marvel-
lous il-
lusion!
Oh
terri-
ble sur-
prise! Oh
mar--
vel-
lous---

-- Oh
marvel-
lous illusion!

LADY S., MRS. P., SIR M., NOTARY, MR. W.

Oh
mar---

---vel-
lous il-
lu----
------
sion! Oh
mar--
--vel-
lous il-
lu---
sion! Oh
mar-vel-
lous illusion!

Oh
mar--

---vel-
lous il-
lu----
------
sion! Oh
mar--
--vel-
lous il-
lu---
sion! Oh
marvel-
lous illusion!

ALEXIS

Oh
marvellous il-
lu-
sion!
Oh
terrible sur-
prise!
Mar-
-vellous il-
lu-----
----
sion! Oh
mar-vel-
lous illusion!

Oh
marvellous il-
lu-
sion!
Oh
terrible sur-
prise!
Mar--
-vellous il-
lu-----
----
sion! Oh
marvel-
lous illusion!

DR. D.

Oh,
mar-
vel-
lous il-
lu----
sion!
Oh
terrible sur-
prise!----

Mar----
vellous il-
lu------

------
sion! Oh
mar-vel-
lous illusion!
Oh
marvellous il-
lu-
sion!
Oh
terrible sur-
prise!---

Mar----
vellous il-
lu------

----
sion! Oh
marvel-
lous illusion!

CHORUS

Oh
marvellous il-
lusion!
Oh
terrible sur-
prise! Oh marvellous il-
lusion! Oh terrible sur-
prise! Oh marvellous il-
lusion! Oh terrible sur-
prise! Oh marvellous il-
lusion! Oh terrible sur-
prise! Oh marvellous il-
lusion! Oh terrible sur-
prise! Oh marvellous il-
lusion! Oh terrible sur-
prise! Oh marvellous il-
lusion! And oh terrible sur-
prise--- Oh
terrible surprise! Oh
marvellous il-
lusion! Oh terrible sur-
prise! Oh marvellous il-
lusion! Oh terrible sur-
prise! Oh marvellous il-
lusion! Oh terrible sur-
prise! Oh marvellous il-
lusion! Oh terrible sur-
prise! Oh marvellous il-
lusion! Oh terrible sur-
prise! Oh marvellous il-
lusion! And oh terrible sur-
prise--- Oh
terrible surprise!

CHORUS   Oh marvellous illusion!

OTHERS   Oh terrible surprise!

CHORUS   Oh marvellous illusion!

ALL   Oh terrible surprise!
What is this strange confusion
That veils their   aching eyes,
        my
That veils their   eyes?
        my

(Those who have partaken of the philtre struggle in vain against its effects, and at the end of the chorus, fall, insensible, on the stage)

END OF ACT I

Act II

SCENE—*Exterior of SIR MARMADUKE'S mansion by moonlight. All the peasantry are discovered asleep on the ground, as at the end of Act I.*

(Enter MR. WELLS, on tiptoes, followed by ALEXIS and ALINE. MR. WELLS carries a dark lantern)

Music No. 15 TRIO AND CHORUS (Aline, Alexis, Mr. Wells, and Chorus)

"'Tis twelve, I think"

TRIO
'Tis twelve, I think,
And at this mystic hour
The magic drink
Should manifest its power.

ALINE	ALEXIS	MR. WELLS
Oh slumb'ring forms,	Oh	Oh
	slum-	slum-
how	b'ring	b'ring
little have	forms,	forms,
ye	how	how
guessed	little have	little have
The	ye	ye
fire that warms,	guess'd	guess'd
	The	The
the		

TRIO
fire that warms each apathetic breast!
Each apathetic breast!

ALEXIS
But stay! my father is not here!

ALINE
And, pray, where is my mother dear?

MR. WELLS
I did not think it meet to see
A dame of lengthy pedigree,
A Baronet and K.C.B.,
A Doctor of divinity,
And that respectable Q.C.
All fast asleep al-fresco-ly,
And so I had them carried home,
And put to bed respectably!
And put to bed respectably!
I trust my conduct meets your approbation!

ALEXIS
Sir, you acted with discrimination,
And showed more delicate appreciation
Than we expect in persons of your station,

ALINE &
MR. WELLS Yes!

ALL 3   It show'd more delicate appreciation

            Than $_{they}^{we}$ expect in persons of $_{my}^{your}$ station!

MR. WELLS   But soft—they waken, one by one,—
            The spell has worked, the deed is done!
            I would suggest that we retire
            While Love, the housemaid, lights her kitchen fire!

ALL 3   While Love, the housemaid, lights her kitchen fire!

            Exeunt MR. WELLS, ALEXIS, and ALINE, on tiptoe, as the villagers
            stretch their arms, yawn, rub their eyes, and sit up.

MEN   Why, where be oi, and what be oi a doin',
            A sleepin' out. just when the dews du rise?

GIRLS   Why that's the very way your health to ruin,
            And don't seem quite respectable likewise!

MEN   *(staring at girls)*. Eh, that's you!
            Only think o' that now!

GIRLS   *(coyly)*. What may you be at, now?
            Tell me, du!

MEN   *(admiringly)*. Eh, what a nose,
            And oh, what eyes, miss!
            Lips like a rose,
            And cheeks likewise, miss!

GIRLS   *(coyly)*. Oi tell you true,
            Which I've never done, sir,
            Oi loike you
            As I never loiked none, sir!

ALL   Eh, but oi du loike you!

MEN   If you'll marry me, I'll dig for you and rake for you!

GIRLS   If you'll marry me, I'll scrub for you and bake for you!

MEN   If you'll marry me, all others I'll forsake for you!

ALL   All this will I du, if you'll marry me!

GIRLS   If you'll marry me, I'll cook for you and brew for you!

MEN   If you'll marry me, I've guineas not a few for you!

GIRLS   If you'll marry me, I'll take you in and du for you!

26

ALL	All this will I du, if you'll marry me!
	All this will I du if you'll marry me!
	Eh! Eh! but I du loike you!

COUNTRY DANCE

(At end of dance, enter CONSTANCE in tears, leading NOTARY, who carries an ear trumpet)

Music No. 16 ENSEMBLE (Constance, Notary, Aline, Alexis, and Chorus)

"Dear friends, take pity on my lot"

ARIA (Constance)

CON.	Dear friends, take pity on my lot,
	My cup is not of nectar!
	I long have lov'd—as who would not?—
	Our kind and rev'rend rector.
	Long years ago my love began,
	So sweetly, yet so sadly,
	But when I saw this plain old man,
	Away my old affection ran—
	I found I lov'd him madly!
	I lov'd him madly!
	Oh!
	(To NOTARY)
	You very, very plain old man,
	I love, I love you madly!
	You very plain old man,
	I love you madly!

| NOTARY | I am a very deaf old man, |
| | And hear you very badly. |

| CHORUS | You very deaf old man, |
| | She loves you madly! |

CON.	I know not why I love him so;
	It is enchantment, surely!
	He's dry and snuffy, deaf and slow,
	Ill-temper'd, weak, and poorly!
	He's ugly, and absurdly dress'd,
	And sixty-seven nearly,
	He's ev'rything that I detest,
	But if the truth must be confess'd,
	I love him very dearly!
	I love him dearly!
	Oh!
	(To NOTARY)
	You're ev'rything that I detest,
	But still I love you dearly!
	You're all that I detest,
	I love you dearly!

NOTARY	I caught that line, but for the rest
	I did not hear it clearly!

CHORUS	You very plain old man,
	She loves you dearly!

(During this verse ALINE and ALEXIS have entered at back, unobserved)

ALEXIS	Oh joy! oh joy!
	The charm works well,
	And all are now united.

ALINE	The blind young boy
	Obeys the spell,
	Their troth they all have plighted.

CON.	Oh, bitter joy!
	No words can tell
	How my poor heart is blighted!
	They'll soon employ a marriage bell
	To say that we're united.
	I do confess
	An anxious care
	My humbled spirit vexes,
	And none will bless
	Example rare
	Of their belov'd Alexis,
	Of their Alexis.

CON.	ALINE & ALEXIS	NOTARY	CHORUS
Oh, bitter joy!	Oh joy! oh joy!	Oh joy! oh joy!	Oh joy! oh joy!
No words can tell	The charm works well,	No words can tell	No words can tell
How my poor heart is blighted!	And all are now united!	My state of mind delighted!	Our state of mind delighted!
They'll soon employ	The blind young boy	They'll soon employ	For girl and boy
A marriage bell	Obeys the spell,	A marriage bell	A marriage bell
To say that we're united.	Their troth they all have plighted.	To say that we're united.	Will say that we're united.
	True happiness reigns ev'rywhere,	True happiness reigns ev'rywhere,	True happiness reigns ev'rywhere,
	And dwells with both the sexes,	And dwells with both the sexes,	And dwells with both the sexes,
And			
none will bless	All will bless	All will bless	All will bless
Example rare	The thoughtful care	Example rare	Example rare
Of their belov'd Alexis.	Of their belov'd Alexis.	Of their belov'd Alexis.	Of their belov'd Alexis.
	True happiness reigns ev'rywhere,	True happiness reigns ev'rywhere,	True happiness reigns ev'rywhere,
	And dwells with both the sexes,	And dwells with both the sexes,	And dwells with both the sexes,
And			

CON. (Contd.)	ALINE & ALEXIS	NOTARY	CHORUS
none will bless	All will bless	All will bless	All will bless
Example rare	the thoughtful care	Example rare	Example rare
Of their belov'd	Of their belov'd	Of their belov'd	Of their belov'd
Alexis.	Alexis.	Alexis.	Alexis.
I do confess			
An anxious care			
My humbled spirit			
vexes,			
And none will bless			
Example rare			
Of their belov'd			
Alexis,			
Of their Alexis.			
Oh, bitter joy!	Oh joy! oh joy!	Oh joy! oh joy!	Oh joy! oh joy!
No words can tell	The charm works well,	No words can tell	No words can tell
How my poor heart	And all are now	My state of mind	Our state of mind
is blighted	united	delighted!	delighted!
They'll soon employ	The blind young boy	They'll soon employ	For girl and boy
A marriage bell	Obeys the spell,	A marriage bell	A marriage bell
To say that we're	Their troth they all have	To say that we're	Will say that we're
united.	plighted.	united.	united.
	True happiness reigns	True happiness reigns	True happiness reigns
	ev'rywhere,	ev'rywhere,	ev'rywhere,
	And dwells with both	And dwells with both	And dwells with both
	the sexes,	the sexes,	the sexes,
And			
none will bless	All will bless	All will bless	All will bless
Example rare	The thoughtful care	Example rare	Example rare
Of their belov'd	Of their belov'd	Of their belov'd	Of their belov'd
Alexis.	Alexis.	Alexis.	Alexis.
	True happiness	True happiness	True happiness
	reigns ev'rywhere	reigns ev'rywhere	reigns ev'rywhere
	And dwells with both	And dwells with both	And dwells with both
	the sexes,	the sexes,	the sexes,
And			
none will bless	All will bless	All will bless	All will bless
Example rare	the thoughtful care	Example rare	Example rare
Of their belov'd	Of their belov'd	Of their belov'd	Of their belov'd
Alexis.	Alexis.	Alexis.	Alexis.

ALL Oh joy! oh joy!
Oh joy! oh joy!
Oh joy! oh joy!
Oh joy! oh joy! oh joy!

(All except ALEXIS and ALINE, exeunt lovingly)

ALINE How joyful they all seem in their new-found happiness! The whole village has paired off in the happiest manner. And yet not a match has been made that the hollow world would not consider ill-advised!

ALEXIS But we are wiser—far wiser—than the world. Observe the good that will become of these ill-assorted unions. The miserly wife will check the reckless expenditure of her too frivolous consort, the wealthy husband will shower innumerable bonnets on his penniless bride, and the young and lively spouse will cheer the declining days of her aged partner with comic songs unceasing!

ALINE	What a delightful prospect for him!
ALEXIS	But one thing remains to be done, that my happiness may be complete. We must drink the philtre ourselves, that I may be assured of your love for ever and ever.
ALINE	Oh Alexis, do you doubt me? Is it necessary that such love as ours should be secured by artificial means? Oh no, no, no!
ALEXIS	My dear Aline, time works terrible changes, and I want to place our love beyond the chance of change.
ALINE	Alexis, it is already far beyond that chance. Have faith in me, for my love can never change!
ALEXIS	Then you absolutely refuse?
ALINE	I do. If you cannot trust me, you have no right to love me—no right to be loved *by* me.
ALEXIS	Enough, Aline, I shall know how to interpret this refusal.

Music No. 17 BALLAD (Alexis)

"It is not love"

ALEXIS	Thou hast the pow'r thy vaunted love
	To sanctify, all doubts above,
	Despite the gath'ring shade;
	To make that love of thine so sure
	That, come what may, it must endure,
	Till time itself shall fade.
	Thy love is but a flow'r
	That fades within the hour;
	If such thy love, oh shame!
	Call it by other name.
	Thy love is but a flow'r
	That fades within the hour;
	If such thy love, oh shame!
	Call it by other name,
	It is not love!
	It is not love!
	Thine is the pow'r, and thine alone,
	To place me on so proud a throne
	That kings might envy me!
	A priceless throne of love untold,
	More rare than orient pearl and gold,
	But no! no!
	Thou would'st be free!
	Such love is like the ray
	That dies within the day:
	If such thy love, oh shame!
	Call it by other name.
	Such love is like the ray

ALEXIS (**Contd.**)	That dies within the day; If such thy love, oh shame! Call it by other name, It is not love, It is not love.

Enter DR. DALY

DR. D.	*(musing)*. It is singular—it is very singular. It has overthrown all my calculations. It is distinctly opposed to the doctrine of averages. I cannot understand it.
ALINE	Dear Dr. Daly, what has puzzled you?
DR. D.	My dear, this village has not hitherto been addicted to marrying and giving in marriage. Hitherto the youths of this village have not been enterprising, and the maidens have been distinctly coy. Judge then of my surprise when I tell you that the whole village came to me in a body just now, and implored me to join them in matrimony with as little delay as possible. Even your excellent father has hinted to me that before very long it is not unlikely that he, also, may change his condition.
ALINE	Oh Alexis—do you hear that? Are you not delighted?
ALEXIS	Yes. I confess that a union between your mother and my father would be a happy circumstance indeed. *(Crossing to* DR. DALY*)*. My dear sir—the news that you bring us is very gratifying.
DR. D.	Yes—still, in my eyes, it has its melancholy side. This universal marrying recalls the happy days—now, alas, gone for ever—when I myself might have—but tush! I am puling. I am too old to marry—and yet, within the last half hour, I have greatly yearned for companionship. I never remarked it before, but the young maidens of this village are very comely. So likewise are the middle-aged. Also the elderly. All are comely—and *(with a deep sigh)* all are engaged!
ALINE	Here comes your father.

Enter SIR MARMADUKE with MRS. PARTLET, arm-in-arm.

ALINE and ALEXIS *(aside)*. Mrs. Partlet!

SIR M.	Dr. Daly, give me joy. Alexis, my dear boy, you will, I am sure, be pleased to hear that my declining days are not unlikely to be solaced by the companionship of this good, virtuous, and amiable woman.
ALEXIS	*(rather taken aback)*. My dear father, this is not altogether what I expected. I am certainly taken somewhat by surprise. Still it can hardly be necessary to assure you that any wife of yours is a mother of mine. *(Aside to* ALINE*)*. It is not quite what I could have wished.
MRS. P.	*(crossing to* ALEXIS*)*. Oh, sir, I entreat your forgiveness. I am aware that socially I am not heverythink that could be desired, nor am I blessed with an abundance of worldly goods, but I can at least confer on your estimable father the great and priceless dowry of a true, tender, and lovin' 'art!

ALEXIS	*(coldly)*. I do not question it. After all, a faithful love is the true source of every earthly joy.
SIR M.	I knew that my boy would not blame his poor father for acting on the impulse of a heart that has never yet misled him. Zorah is not perhaps what the world calls beautiful—
DR. D.	Still she is comely—distinctly comely! *(Sighs)*.
ALINE	Zorah is very good, and very clean, and honest: and quite, quite sober in her habits, and that is worth far more than beauty, dear Sir Marmaduke.
DR. D.	Yes; beauty will fade and perish, but personal cleanliness is practically undying, for it can be renewed whenever it discovers symptoms of decay. My dear Sir Marmaduke, I heartily congratulate you. *(Sighs)*.

Music No. 18 QUINTET (Aline, Mrs. Partlet (Zorah), Alexis, Dr. Daly, & Sir Marmaduke)

"I rejoice that it's decided"

ALEXIS	I rejoice that it's decided, Happy now will be his life, For my father is provided With a kind and tender wife.
ENSEMBLE	She will tend him, nurse him, mend him, Air his linen, dry his tears; Bless the thoughtful fates that send him Such a wife to soothe his years!
ALINE	No young giddy thoughtless maiden, Full of graces, airs, and jeers— But a sober widow, laden With the weight of fifty years!
SIR M.	No highborn exacting beauty, Blazing like a jewelled sun— But a wife who'll do her duty, As that duty should be done!
ENSEMBLE	She will tend him, nurse him, mend him, Air his linen, dry his tears; Bless the thoughtful fates that send him Such a wife to soothe his years!
MRS. P.	I'm no saucy minx and giddy— Hussies such as them abound— But a clean and tidy widdy Well be-known for miles around!
DR. D.	All the village now have mated, And are happy as can be; I to live alone am fated, No one left to marry me.

ALINE, MRS. P.,
ALEXIS, SIR M. No one left to marry him

ENSEMBLE She will tend him, nurse him, mend him,
Air his linen, dry his tears,
Bless the thoughtful fates that send him
Such a wife to soothe his years

ALINE, MRS. PARTLET	ALEXIS, DR. DALY	SIR MARMADUKE
	Bless the	
	thoughtful fates	Such
	that	a
	send him	wife
Such	Such	
a	a	to
wife to	wife to	soothe
soothe his	soothe his	his
years,	years,	years, Such a
Such		wife,
a	Such a	Such a
wife to soothe his years.	wife to soothe his years.	wife to soothe his years.

Exit SIR MARMADUKE, with MRS. PARTLET, and ALINE, with ALEXIS. DR. DALY looks after them sentimentally, then exit with a sigh. Enter MR. WELLS.

Music No. 19 RECIT. and DUET (Lady Sangazure and Mr. Wells)

"Oh, I have wrought much evil with my spells!"

RECITATIVE—MR. WELLS

Oh, I have wrought much evil with my spells!
And ill I can't undo!
This is too bad of you, J. W. Wells—
What wrong have they done you?
And see—another love-lorn lady comes—
Alas, poor stricken dame!
A gentle pensiveness her life benumbs—
And mine, alone, the blame!

LADY SANGAZURE enters. She is very melancholy.

LADY S. Alas! ah me! and well-a-day!
I sigh for love, and well I may.
For I am very old and gray.
But stay!

(Sees MR. WELLS, and becomes fascinated by him)

RECITATIVE

LADY S. What is this fairy form I see before me?

MR. WELLS	Oh horrible!—she's going to adore me! This last catastrophe is overpowering!
LADY S.	Why do you glare at me with visage low'ring? For pity's sake recoil not thus from me!
MR. WELLS	My lady, leave me—this can never be!

DUET—LADY SANGAZURE and MR. WELLS

MR. WELLS	Hate me! I drop my H's—have through life!
LADY S.	Love me! I'll drop them too!
MR. WELLS	Hate me! I always eat peas with a knife!
LADY S.	Love me! I'll eat like you!
MR. WELLS	Hate me! I often roll down One Tree Hill!
LADY S.	Love me! I'll meet you there!
MR. WELLS	Hate me! I sometimes go to Rosherville!
LADY S.	Love me! that joy I'll share! Love me! my prejudices I'll for ever drop!
MR. WELLS	Hate me! that's not enough!
LADY S.	Love me! I'll come and help you in the shop!
MR. WELLS	Hate me! the life is rough!
LADY S.	Love me! my grammar I will all forswear!
MR. WELLS	Hate me! abjure my lot!
LADY S.	Love me! I'll stick sunflowers in my hair!
MR. WELLS	Hate me! they'll suit you not!

RECITATIVE—MR. WELLS
At what I am going to say be not enraged—
I may not love you—for I am engaged!

LADY S.	*(horrified)*. Engaged! engaged!
MR. WELLS	Engaged! To a maiden fair, With bright brown hair, And a sweet and simple smile, Who waits for me By the sounding sea, On a South Pacific isle.

MR. WELLS *(aside)*. A lie! No maiden waits me there!

LADY S. *(mournfully)*. She has bright brown hair!

MR. WELLS *(aside)*. A lie! No maiden smiles on me!

LADY S. *(mournfully)*. By the sounding sea!

BOTH The sounding sea!

LADY S. Oh agony, rage, despair!
The maiden has bright brown hair,
And mine is as white as snow!
False man, it will be your fault
If I go to my family vault,
And bury my life-long woe!

MR. WELLS Oh agony, rage, despair!
Oh where will this end? oh where?
I should very much like to know!
It will certainly be my fault
If she goes to her family vault,
To bury her life-long woe!

LADY SANGAZURE	MR. WELLS
False man, it	
will	'Twill
be	certain-
your	ly
fault if	be
I	my
go to my family	fault
vault, And bury my	If she goes to her
life-	fami-
long woe!	ly vault!
The family vault,	
	The vault,
the family vault,	
	the fa-
The fa-	
mily vault,	mily vault,
	The family vault,
The vault,	
	the family vault,
the vault,	
	The family vault,
the fa-	
	the fa-
mily vault,	mily vault,
	The family vault,
The vault,	
	the family vault,

LADY SANGAZURE (Contd.)	MR. WELLS (Contd.)
the vault,	
	The family vault,
Yes, the family vault!	Yes, the family vault!

(Exit LADY SANGAZURE, in great anguish, accompanied by MR. WELLS. Enter ALINE)

Music No. 20 RECIT. AND AIR (Aline)

"Alexis! Doubt me not, my loved one!"

RECITATIVE—ALINE

Alexis! Doubt me not, my loved one! See,
Thine uttered will is sovereign law to me!
All fear—all thought of ill I cast away!
It is my darling's will, and I obey!

(She drinks the philtre)

The fearful deed is done,
My love is near!
I go to meet my own
In trembling fear!
If o'er us aught of ill
Should cast a shade,
It was my darling's will,
And I obey'd! and I obey'd!

(As ALINE is going off, she sees DR. DALY, entering pensively. He is playing on a flageolet. Under the influence of the spell she at once becomes strangely fascinated by him, and exhibits every symptom of being hopelessly in love with him.)

Music No. 21 SONG (Dr. Daly)

"Engaged to So-and-so"

DR. D. Oh, my voice is sad and low,
And with timid step I go—
For with load of love o'erladen
I enquire of ev'ry maiden,
"Will you wed me, little lady,
Will you share my cottage shady?"
Little lady answers "No! No! No!"
"Thank you for your kindly proffer—
Good your heart, and full your coffer:
Yet, I must decline your offer—
I'm engag'd to So-and-so!" *(flageolet solo)*.
So-and-so! So-and-so! *(flageolet solo)*.
So-and-so! So-and-so! *(flageolet solo)*.

DR. D.	She's engag'd to So-and-so!
(Contd.)	What a rogue young hearts to pillage!
	What a worker on Love's tillage!
	Ev'ry maiden in the village
	Is engag'd to So-and-so! *(flageolet solo)*
	So-and-so! So-and-so! *(flageolet solo)*
	So-and-so! So-and-so! *(flageolet solo)*
	All engag'd to So-and-so!

(At the end of the song DR. DALY sees ALINE, and, under the influence of the potion, falls in love with her.)

Music No. 22 ENSEMBLE (Aline, Alexis, Dr. Daly, and Chorus)

"Oh, joyous boon! oh, mad delight!"

ALINE	DR. DALY
Oh, joyous boon! oh, mad delight!	Oh, joyous boon! oh, mad delight!
Oh, sun and moon! oh, day and night!	Oh, sun and moon! oh, day and night!
Rejoice, rejoice ---	Rejoice, ---
---------	rejoice with
with	
me!	me!
Proclaim our joy, ye birds above—	Proclaim our joy, ye birds above—
Ye brooklets murmur forth our love,	Ye brooklets murmur forth our love,
In choral ecstacy.	In choral ecstacy.
	Oh, joyous boon!
Oh, mad delight!	
	Oh, sun and moon!
Oh, day and night!	

ALINE	Rejoice with me, Rejoice with me,
& DR. D.	Rejoice, rejoice with me!

Enter ALEXIS

ALEXIS	*(with rapture)*. Aline, my only love, my happiness!
	The philtre—you have tasted it?

ALINE	*(with confusion)*. Yes! Yes!

ALEXIS	Oh, joy, mine, mine for ever, and for ever!

(Embraces her)

ALINE	Alexis, don't do that—you must not!

(DR. DALY interposes between them)

ALEXIS	*(amazed)*. Why?

37

DUET—ALINE and DR. DALY

ALINE   Alas! that lovers thus should meet:
Oh pity me!
Oh, charge me not with cold deceit;
Oh pity, pity me!
You bade me drink—with trembling awe.
I drank, and, by the potion's law
I lov'd the very first I saw!
Oh pity, pity me!

DR. D.   My dear young friend, consoled be—
We pity, pity you.
In this I'm not an agent free—
We pity, pity you.
Some most extraordinary spell,
O'er us has cast its magic fell—
The consequence I need not tell.
We pity, pity you.

ALEXIS   Some most extraordinary spell,

ALL THREE   O'er $\begin{smallmatrix}\text{them}\\\text{us}\end{smallmatrix}$ hath cast its magic fell—

ALEXIS   *(furiously)* False one, begone! I spurn thee!
To thy new lover turn thee!
Thy perfidy all men shall know

ALINE   *(wildly)*. I could not help it!

ALEXIS   *(calling off)*. Come one, come all!

DR. D.   We could not help it!

ALEXIS   *(calling off)*. Obey my call!

ALINE *(wildly)*	**ALEXIS** *(Calling off)*	**DR. DALY**
		We could
I could not		
help		not
it!		
	Come,	
	hither,	help
	run!	it!
I		
could not		We
help it!		could
		not
I		
could not	Come,	
help it!	ev-	help
	'ry	
Oh, a-	one,	it! A-
las!	come!	las!

38

(Enter all the characters except LADY SANGAZURE and MR. WELLS)

CHORUS Oh, what is the matter, and what is the clatter?
He's glowering at her, and threatens a blow!
Oh, why does he batter the girl he did flatter?
And why does the latter recoil from him

CHORUS	ALEXIS	OTHERS
so? Oh, what is the matter, and	Oh, thus	Oh, why
what is the	do	does
clatter? Oh,	I	he
why does he batter the girl he did flatter? And why does the latter	bat- ter, And thus does the latter	bat- ter And why does the latter
recoil from him so?	recoil from me so?	recoil from him so?
Why does the latter	Thus does the latter	Why does the latter
recoil from him so?	recoil from me so?	recoil from him so?

Music No. 23 RECIT. (Alexis)

"Prepare for sad surprises"

ALEXIS Prepare for sad surprises—
My love Aline despises!
No thought of sorrow shames her—
Another lover claims her!
Be his, false girl, for better or for worse—
But, ere you leave me, may a lover's curse—

DR. D. *(coming forward)*. Hold! Be just. This poor child drank the philtre at your instance. She hurried off to meet you—but, most unhappily, she met me instead. As you had administered the potion to both of us, the result was inevitable. But fear nothing from me—I will be no man's rival. I shall quit the country at once—and bury my sorrow in the congenial gloom of a Colonial Bishopric.

ALEXIS My excellent old friend! *(Taking his hand—then turning to* MR. WELLS, *who has entered with* LADY SANGAZURE.) Oh, Mr. Wells, what, what is to be done?

MR. WELLS I do not know—and yet—there is one means by which this spell may be removed.

ALEXIS Name it—oh name it!

MR. WELLS Or you or I, must yield up his life to Ahrimanes. I would rather it were you. I should have no hesitation in sacrificing my own life to spare yours, but we take stock next week, and it would not be fair on the Co.

ALEXIS	True. Well, I am ready!

ALINE	No, no—Alexis—it must not be! Mr. Wells, if he must die that all may be restored to their old loves, what is to become of me? I should be left out in the cold, with no love to be restored to!

MR. WELLS	True—I did not think of that. *(To the others.)* My friends, I appeal to you, and I will leave the decision in your hands.

Music No. 24 FINALE

"Or he or I must die"

MR. WELLS	Or he, or I Must die! Which shall it be? Reply!

SIR M.	Die thou! Thou art the cause of all offending!

DR. D.	Die thou! Yield thou to this decree unbending!

ALL	Die thou! die thou! die thou!

MR. WELLS	So be it! I submit! My fate is sealed. To popular opinion thus I yield!

(**Falls on trap C.**)

Be happy all—leave me to my despair—
I go—it matters not with whom—or where!

(**Gong**)

All quit their present partners, and rejoin their old lovers. SIR MARMADUKE leaves MRS. PARTLET and goes to LADY SANGAZURE. ALINE leaves DR. DALY and goes to ALEXIS. DR. DALY leaves ALINE and goes to CONSTANCE. NOTARY leaves CONSTANCE and goes to MRS. PARTLET. All the chorus make a corresponding change.

ALL

MEN	Oh my adored one!

GIRLS	Beloved boy!

MEN	Ecstatic rapture!

GIRLS	Unmingled joy!

(**They embrace**)

SIR M.   Come to my mansion, all of you! At least
                We'll crown our rapture with another feast!

ALINE, LADY SANGAZURE, ALEXIS, SIR MARMADUKE

Now to the banquet we press,
Now for the eggs and the ham!
Now for the mustard and cress,
Now for the strawberry jam!

CONSTANCE, MRS. PARTLET, VICAR, & NOTARY

Now for the rollicking bun!
Now for the muffin and toast,
And now for the gay Sally Lunn!
Now for the muffin and toast,
And now for the gay Sally Lunn!

ENSEMBLE   The eggs and the ham
             And the strawberry jam,
             The rollicking bun
             And the gay Sally Lunn!

ALINE, CON., 1st SOPRANOS	ALL OTHERS
The	The
eggs,	eggs and the ham, And the strawberry jam,
The	The
ham,	rollicking bun And the gay Sally Lunn!

ENSEMBLE   The eggs and the ham
             And the strawberry jam
             And the rollicking bun!
             The rollicking bun
             And the gay Sally Lunn,
             And the strawberry jam,

WOMEN	MEN
jam,	
	bun,
jam,	
	bun,
Oh! the strawberry, strawberry jam,	Oh! the strawberry, strawberry jam,
bun,	
	jam,
bun,	
	jam,

ENSEMBLE   Oh! the rollicking, rollicking bun!

(General Dance)

(During the symphony MR. WELLS sinks through trap, amid red fire)
THE END